DEPRESSION IS A WEAPON USED BY THE ENEMY TO DESTROY THE STRONG

By Oliviah Mona

Depression is a Weapon used by
the Enemy to Destroy the Strong

Published by Oliviah Mona

Boksburg, South Africa

monanokuthula@yahoo.com

ISBN 978-1-83492-225-6

eISBN 978-1-83492-226-3

2 4 6 8 10 9 7 5 3 1

Layout and cover design by Boutique Books

INTENT OF THIS BOOK

This book is for everyone who would like to get an insight into what depression is. What causes depression? How does God deliver us from depression? It is mainly focused on the power of God in all circumstances. When you trust in God by believing His Word concerning your life, you will overcome depression and conquer all that the enemy brings your way. This book advises you on how to pray when you are experiencing depression, especially when you don't even feel like praying at all.

The truth is that in this life we often face unexpected situations for which we are not prepared. Depending on the situation and your state of mind at the time, you might get stressed, anxious, depressed or experience other emotions. It is at this time that God gives you His Peace and assures you that He has everything under control. You might not be experiencing depression yourself right now, but if you want to know more about God's Great power and might, this is the right book for you.

CONTENTS

INTRODUCTION

To start off, we will first go through some important definitions that will help us understand the content of this book better. The definitions are as follows:

Depression is defined as a state of mind producing serious, long-term lowering of enjoyment of life or the inability to visualise a happy future.

Mind is an element of a person that enables them to be aware of the world and their experiences. It enables them to think and feel. The mind is the capability of consciousness and thought.

Thought is an idea or opinion produced by thinking or occurring suddenly in the mind.

The enemy is Satan or the devil. (The words enemy/Satan/devil are used interchangeably in the content of this book.)

CHAPTER 1

THE MIND

The mind is the greatest part of a person; it is an incredible organ of the body. Everything is possible in the mind. When you believe and are determined in your mind that something is possible, then it is already done. All you need to do is to execute it. Nothing can change your mind once you believe in something. That is what it takes: *"believing".* Then things will happen as you believe.

If the mind is not determined and you do not believe or you have doubts, it doesn't matter how hard you try to do or achieve something, you are most likely to fail at it. It will fail in your mind first when you think about it. It takes determination in your mind and believing in your heart for you to execute things into existence in this physical world.

The mind works in a different dynamic and if it believes in something, whether good or bad, it executes it based on that person's belief. It is the centre of possibilities, where everything is executed. A person succeeds or fails in the mind first, before they succeed or fail in real life. When you fail an exam, fail in a job interview or when your presentation at school or at work goes badly, you didn't fail at the time that these things happened. Instead, you failed them in the mind first, when you thought about them. The doubt or lack of confidence you had when you thought of the exam, the interview or the presentation resulted in failure in the end.

When an idea comes to your mind, and you are convinced that you will execute it successfully, your results will be as per your belief. Success and failure are achieved in the mind first, before they can be achieved in real life. You win in the mind first, before you win in real life.

CHAPTER 2

WHY IS THE MIND ATTACKED?

The mind has no limitations. According to the mind, nothing is impossible. You only need to believe, and things happen as per your belief. When the mind is attacked, your entire belief system is compromised. Instead of believing you can achieve certain things in your life, you start believing that you can't achieve them. This negative belief is often accompanied by a lot of reasons that convince you that you really can't.

The enemy – **Satan, also called the devil** – is fully aware that the mind is the greatest weapon in a human. So, if he attacks the mind, he knows that there is a high chance that he might win. He executes this attack through **deception**. The enemy deceives you into believing the lies that he presents to you about something, and he leaves you to destroy yourself, your future, your destiny through how you think after he lied to you. You end up overthinking, and his lies start to penetrate your mind and drain you.

When you think of it, all the devil does is to bring negative thoughts or lies about things or situations in our lives daily, until we believe those lies and we are convinced that they are true. Once we believe his lies, we act according to that belief and destroy ourselves by overthinking and all kinds of emotional wracking.

The devil will not only use one lie to convince you about something negative because he knows that the mind is powerful and that it naturally thinks positively. So, he will come up with his own *"facts"* or *"track record"* of occurrences, which happened either in your life or in your family. The enemy goes as far as tracking a certain family from generation to generation to build his evidence to destroy a particular individual so that, when he presents this information to the individual, his lies sound like the truth. The lies sound like facts and the person gets convinced. John 10:10 says **"the thief's purpose (Satan) is to steal, kill and destroy. My purpose (Jesus) is to give them a rich and satisfying life."**

People usually endure physical attacks such as injury or sickness much better than they endure the attack on the mind. This is because they have seen or heard of a lot of people who got injured in car accidents or those who got sick, and they also heard of them getting well and healthy again. This sets their minds at ease when they face such situations themselves. Even if they might also be affected emotionally and mentally when they get sick or injured, there is a lot of evidence that people have recovered from such circumstances. This somehow also encourages them to have hope that they will get well soon too. They tell themselves, "I need to take my medication as required and I will be healed".

However, when it comes to the attack of the mind, it is not an easy one to overcome. In our society, depression is often taken lightly and ridiculed or taken as a weakness. Meanwhile, it is the greatest and most powerful attack that a person can experience. You may wonder, if depression is that unimportant and a weakness, how come people of different ages, races, nationalities, social statuses (the poor and the rich alike) take their lives almost every day. If it was based on social status, only poor people would be killing themselves due to depression, but that is not the case.

Depression can attack any person at any point and time of their lives. It could be caused by the loss of a loved one, unemployment, sickness, financial struggles, loss of a job, etc. It could even be a spiritual attack. Depression could be caused by different circumstances for different people.

Coming back to the mind, the mind can also be defined as "**a house of all possibilities**". In the mind there is no limitation, no impossibility and all things are possible. If you are ready for something in your life – it can be a new job, a business, marriage or anything else – your mind must be determined on it first; then you will succeed in it.

If you have a good idea or a goal and you tell yourself that "**no matter what, I will achieve it**", your mind will focus only on achieving that goal. Even if challenges come along the way, they will not stop you from achieving your goal. That is how things work when your mind is determined.

The reason why the enemy attacks the mind with depression and anxiety is because he knows that your mind is the most powerful weapon you have to achieve all you want to achieve in life. If he brings negativity to your mind, his intentions are not to bring you temporary distraction, but rather permanent distraction that will eventually destroy your life. His intentions are to ensure that you achieve nothing in your life. He intends to depress you in such a way that every day when you wake up in the morning, you wake up with a defeated mindset.

The enemy's intention is to ensure that there is always something negative that your mind is focused on, which distracts you from seeing the good, positive things in your life. Every day you start seeing yourself as a failure, a nobody, someone who does not deserve to live. The enemy will make you feel like God doesn't love you. Some he will make feel like they were born by mistake. He does all these things to steal your destiny from you. It doesn't end with him stealing your destiny: he intends to kill you and destroy your life completely.

It is not that you are weak when you get attacked with the spirit of depression. The enemy will try other things first to destroy you, and if they don't work, he will then try to destroy you through depression: by attacking your mind. Remember, your mind is a house of all possibilities, so if the mind is attacked your entire belief system is affected. The enemy doesn't rest; he is at work every day trying to steal people's destinies. He works so hard to weaken you (your mind) through the spirit of depression once he has found something negative to disturb your mind with.

Once he finds that one thing that puts you down and drives your mind to think negatively, he uses it every day to destroy you and shame you. But there is a way out of such a situation. Jesus Christ is His Name. Jesus died for you to have freedom, not only from sin but from every kind of captivity and limitation that Satan uses to stop you from living the abundant life Jesus gave you through His death and resurrection.

After Jesus rose from death, He said, "**I have been given all authority in heaven and on earth**" (Matthew 28:18). This means that there is nothing that can't be done or undone through **Jesus Christ**. With Jesus on your side, there is nothing you can't achieve or overcome because **He has all power in heaven and on earth**.

If you have Jesus in your life as your Lord and Saviour, then you have authority over all power of the enemy. In Luke 10:19, the Word of God says, "**I have given you authority over all the power of the enemy, and you can walk among snakes and**

scorpions and crush them. Nothing will injure you." This is the authority that Jesus Christ gave you: **there is no power that the enemy can use against you that you cannot overcome through Jesus Christ**. You have already overcome. The enemy knows the kind of authority you have through Jesus, which is why every day he is at work with no rest trying to defeat you.

CHAPTER 3

HOW DOES THE ENEMY DEFEAT YOU THROUGH DEPRESSION?

At the beginning of this book, a definition of what depression is was provided. To recap, depression was defined as a state of mind producing serious long-term lowering of enjoyment of life or the inability to visualise a happy future. When you are depressed, all you can think about is the one negative thing that lowers you down and makes you not visualise a happy future for yourself. This is a trick the enemy uses to destroy you – or rather, to make you destroy yourself by overthinking.

The enemy is fighting the kingdom of God (every child of God) entirely. He is not necessarily fighting you at a personal level (that is, he is not attacking you because of something you did to him). He is fighting the destiny God put in you, which is intended to fulfil the Will of God. Your destiny is intended to bring **glory** to God, and that is why the enemy is fighting you. He attacks anything that brings glory to God, and he will only attack you if there is a reason to fight you. This is stopping you from fulfilling your destiny.

Anything and everything that brings glory to God, the enemy fights. This is why he fights children from birth, children at schools, people in their homes, workplaces, marriages, businesses and so on: to stop their lives from bringing glory to God. Literally, he fights anyone who has the potential to glorify God. To repeat, the enemy is fighting the kingdom of God entirely; it is not a personal attack. This is a spiritual attack, and it is way bigger and deeper than you might think.

Depression is a spiritual attack that is intended to destroy the strong. It takes the enemy a long time to study you so well to understand your strengths and weaknesses. He tries a lot of different techniques before he can get you to a state of depression. This can take years, until he finds that one thing that weakens you to a point of no motivation. Once he finds that one thing, he will use it against you throughout your life until you overcome it.

Unfortunately, this period is not an easy one for the person being attacked by the enemy. Some people sadly don't manage to overcome this kind of attack (depression) and they end up taking their own lives. In our society, people who end up taking their own lives are considered to be *weak people* because it is perceived that depression is for the weak.

Most people even say, if only the people who took their own lives had talked about what troubled them instead of resorting to death. The truth is that most people who are depressed talk about what bothers them more than we think. They mention what is troubling their minds to different people at different times, hoping to get help, but most of the time the people they talk to don't take them seriously, or they take their problems lightly or they start gossiping about the person's problems.

To give an insight into our society, how it works is that when people who are depressed open up about it, they are laughed at and gossiped about. This leads the people who are depressed to end up deciding that, no matter how hard it gets, they will deal with what they are experiencing by themselves.

Eventually, when things get severe, well, they speak about it but they become a joke and laughingstock. They are called weak and all other disgraceful names. So, they end up thinking that death by ending their own lives is the only way they can get *"rest"*. They believe that such a decision will put an end to their misery. Now, this is the sad ending of depression. The sad part is that such a powerful attack *(depression)* in society is not talked about, and people who experience it are laughed at. This could be due to a lack of knowledge in society about depression itself, but yeah, it is sad.

Truly speaking, lucky are those who never get to experience depression throughout their entire lives because they might not be stretched to the last point of strength that their minds can reach. Often, if a person is depressed and if they are Christian, they are asked questions like, "Do you pray about it?" Some people simply say, "Don't think about it," and in fact the suggestions you get are things you have already tried more than once without succeeding in overcoming the depression.

However, there is a way out of depression that works. **God** is the way out! If you surrender everything to God through Jesus Christ –*"Surrender what depresses you to God"* – He is **Faithful** and He will deliver you. The one thing about God amongst other things about Him, is that He **never** fails.

CHAPTER 4

WHAT TECHNIQUES DOES THE ENEMY USE TO GET A PERSON DEPRESSED?

It is important to note that the enemy does not always use the same technique when he attacks people. He uses different techniques on different people, otherwise his techniques will not work. For some people, especially teenagers, he may use their physical appearance to make them insecure about themselves. He makes the targeted person aware of all the features they don't like about themselves and ensures that others always point those features out to validate that they are not beautiful. For some people, this might not be an issue: they can easily reassure themselves that they know they are beautiful. However, for others it can break them down and hurt them badly.

For some people, he may use unemployment to depress them. The person might have been unemployed for a long time and be at a point where they are losing hope. The enemy can use this as an opportunity to attack the person's mind with negativity. Some people who are unemployed may still have hope and believe that they will get a job soon, but once the enemy targets such people he will start lying to them, saying all sorts of things to get them discouraged to a point where they believe they will never get employed. He whispers these lies to them until they fall into the depression trap.

For some people, being unemployed is not the worst for them. They believe that at the right time God will give them the job they deserve. Even if the enemy tries to lie to them, they

stubbornly believe that God will come through with a job for them. For such people, the enemy will look for something else. He can make some people feel like they are not loved, either by their families or by everyone around them in general. He uses all sorts of tricks to make the person believe that this is true while it is not.

For some people who seem to be on track in life career-wise, health-wise, financially and so on, the enemy can use infertility in their marriage to get them depressed. Some people can endure infertility a bit better, but for others at some point, especially if they have been dealing with infertility for a long time, it might wear them down.

About some people he might tell lies (make false accusations), while he knows that everything said about the person is not true. In this instance, stories about the person will be flying around while the person talked about doesn't know where they come from. This causes the person to be undermined, disrespected, disgraced and humiliated. It affects their self-confidence and how they feel about themselves, and eventually they get depressed.

The goal of the enemy when he attacks a person with depression is to ensure that the person is miserable: that they feel futureless and life becomes meaningless to them. Taking that into consideration, the enemy will not attack you with something you can easily overcome within a few days, weeks or months. He plans to make your life miserable until you die; hence, he works hard to find something that will knock your positive, confident mind to the core and change your life completely.

The one thing about the enemy is that he studies a person's entire life. That might sound exaggerated, but it is true. He

watches their life entirely and observes what they love, what they hate, what makes them angry, what makes them happy, what their weaknesses are, their strengths and all that. His reason for doing this is so he can plan a proper attack against the person: a strategic attack. He ensures that the attack against the person will certainly destroy them. To add to this, he can study the person's entire family, the generations and their entire bloodline, just to have a strategic attack against them or even against their entire family. That is how determined he is.

CHAPTER 5

THERE IS LIGHT AT THE END OF THE TUNNEL

Above all the emotions, the pain and brokenness, there is God who is **faithful**. God's plans for your life are for your good and not for disaster, to give you a future and a hope (Jeremiah 29:11). He knew you before you were formed in your mother's womb. Before you were born, He destined you (Jeremiah 1:5) for greatness which is intended for His glory. So, above all, God is still in charge! What you need to do is to surrender everything unto Him, trust Him and thank Him that He will fulfil the destiny He has for you.

As mentioned earlier in this book, the mind is a powerful part in a person and from there all things are possible. This is why, when the mind is attacked, the whole body is affected. When the enemy attacks the body with sickness or any other physical harm, the mind still functions as it should. So, you can still think properly, dream, believe and execute great things in your life. But when the mind is what is affected, your entire body is affected. This also affects your dreams and goals. At this time a lot of negativity kicks in.

But God is not a man, He does not lie. He is not human. He does not change His mind. He never speaks and then fails to act on His Word. He never promises and then does not carry His promises through (Numbers 23:19).

When you get attacked by depression, never make the mistake of trying to deal with it by yourself. Give it to God and He will handle it. God created you. He is responsible for your life

and that includes the state of your mind. After all, He created the mind and made it function the way it does. So, you should rather give all matters that pertain to you to God. He is in charge of your life.

In Isaiah 43:4, God says, "**You are precious to me, you are honoured, and I love you**". That is all you need: God's unfailing love. When you feel weak, pray. Ask God to give you strength for you to remain standing in **faith**. In Isaiah 43:13, God says, "**From eternity to eternity I am God. No one can snatch anyone out of my hand. No one can undo what I have done**". This is assurance for you that, if your life is in God's hands, no one can snatch you out of **His hands. You are safe forever**. He will **always protect** you, and **He will never ever fail you**.

CHAPTER 6

GOD CARED FOR YOU SINCE YOU WERE BORN

In Isaiah 46:3, God says "**I cared for you since you were born**". He says "**Yes, I carried you before you were born**". What does this mean? It means that, even before your parents thought of having a child – and of course they never knew it would be you – God already knew you. God carried you while you were in your mother's womb and, from the day you were born to this day, He has cared for you.

Now, let's take a moment and break this down: from the time a child is conceived to the time they are born, a lot can happen. Some babies die after a few days, weeks or months of being conceived; some a few months before birth and some die on the day of birth due to complications.

What does it mean when God says, "**I carried you before you were born**". It means that from the time He thought about creating you, He ensured that you would live from then. It means that He formed you in your mother's womb and carried you from then until the day and time when you were born. Physically, it was your mother who carried you throughout the pregnancy period, but in the spirit God was the one carrying you and protecting you all that time.

God ensured that you were born safely. He did not stop there but He also protected you from the day you were born to this day. He doesn't miss even a single moment of your life. Whether you are aware of it or not, God is always there with you, and for

you. Now, if He cares about you this much, how can He let you be miserable and defeated?

In Isaiah 46:4, God says, "**I will be your God throughout your lifetime, until your hair is white with age. I made you and I will care for you. I will carry you along and save you**". In this verse, God is taking full responsibility for your life. He is saying, "Because I chose to create you, I will be your God throughout your life."

If God is in charge of your life, then how can He leave you alone to deal with depression? There is no way that God can leave you to deal with the attack on your mind alone. He will never let you fight such a battle alone.

The one thing you need to do is to **surrender** it to Him and **trust** Him. You need to trust in the **truth** that God **never** fails. He will carry you through it. He will fight for you and give you victory. After all, any battle pertaining to you, whether small or big, belongs to Him. So, surrender everything to God (what bothers your heart, your mind, your body, etc.) and get some rest. He will certainly give you victory. He will **never** fail you. **Trust** Him and He will see you through it victoriously.

CHAPTER 7

GOD WORKS IN SILENCE

If you have been on this journey with God for a while, you should be aware by now that God works in silence. A lot of people can agree that this is a difficult part in any challenge or battle. This is because at this time, even if you know that God has heard your prayers, it feels like He hasn't. At this time, you don't know what He is doing about your request; you don't know exactly when He is planning to deliver you completely and how He will do it.

The truth be told, the waiting period while God is working in silence is painful. Often you wonder, is God even going to deliver me? Is He really going to save me? This is mostly due to the prolonged period of the battle or challenge. You might be able to stand and wait for a period of three years, for example, praying for God to deliver you from something, but once the period becomes four, five, six, seven years, you might start getting weary and losing hope.

Unfortunately, this part of the process cannot be skipped, bypassed or fast-tracked. This is where **faith** comes in. It is where you need to ask for a lot of strength daily from God to be strong and stand firm. Honestly, it is very easy to give up at this point because it feels like God is watching you suffer while He is doing nothing about it.

But remember, even Jesus Christ could not bypass this stage. In Luke 22:42, Jesus asked God to take the cup of suffering from Him (His brutal death). Jesus didn't make this request once. The bible says He asked God to remove the cup of suffering from Him

three times, but God didn't give a response at the time. God did not say a single word after Jesus prayed. Jesus still went through the suffering process, and He was crucified.

This shows that God works that way, and He makes no exceptions. But what we also learn from this verse is that at the end of His prayer, Jesus said, "**Not my will, but Yours be done**". Jesus surrendered to the Will of God and the Will of God was done. The main reason Jesus came to earth was to save us through His death and His resurrection. Yes, Jesus died, but He rose on the third day as God promised. He is still **alive,** even today.

At the end, the Will of God will prevail in your life. Not the will of the enemy. **Trust** God! While waiting in your situation, remember one thing: **God Never Fails**. So, whether you see it or not, God is working things out for your good. He is fighting for you, and you have already won. During God's silence, keep **reading** His Word and declaring it in your life. Keep **praying**, keep **fasting** (when God commands you to and at your own initiative). Keep **praising** God! He has **already** won the battle for you. Know that He is a **faithful** God Who **never** fails.

CHAPTER 8

GOD KNEW YOU BEFORE YOU WERE FORMED

od says, "**I knew you before I formed you in your mother's womb. Before you were born, I set you apart and appointed you as my prophet to the nations**" (Jeremiah 1:5). This information goes beyond understanding! The truth is that, before you were born, God already knew you and He had already destined you.

As previously quoted from Isaiah 46:3, God said, "**I carried you before you were born**". This means that there is a chance that you could have not been born, if God had not carried you. God ensured that you were born safely. Before you met the people on earth who became your family, friends or enemies, God was already protecting you. If He was able to carry you and protect you before you were born, how can He not be able to protect and save you now?

Furthermore, God has been by your side from the day you were born to this day. There is no point in your life where He ever left you. He was always with you. He was with you in shame, pain, hurt, humiliation, disgrace, betrayal, hatred, in good times and in heartbreaking moments of your life. God was always by your side, and He still is. To add to this, looking at Jesus Christ, He was God (Philippians 2:6), but when He had to die, He suffered a very painful and disgraceful death.

People, being sinners, couldn't bear the kind of death Jesus had to bear. God was with Jesus the whole time and in everything that He had to bear. The Will of God was fulfilled throughout the

life of Jesus Christ. God did not take the cup of suffering from Jesus to save Him from pain because the pain was part of the Will of God. God was with Jesus the whole time, while God's Will was being fulfilled through Jesus' life. The lives of many people were saved through the death and resurrection of Jesus Christ, and this was God's plan from the beginning.

Again, whether you are aware of it or not, God is always with you in that situation you are facing right now. The situation is very painful, but He is with you in it. Whatever troubles you, know that God is with you in it. Remember, God **never** fails, so victory is already yours in every situation. Trust God and His purpose, because He will fulfil His purpose for your life (Philippians 1:6).

CHAPTER 9

GOD NEVER FAILS!

God would not carry you from before you were born, only to fail you now. Although you were already His, the moment you give your life to Him (believed in your heart and confessed with your mouth that Jesus Christ is the Lord), He takes charge of your life entirely. Your life becomes about Him, not you. This means that your life is a representative of God and God can never fail Himself. Your life is intended to bring glory to God. If you face a period of shame, be aware that, since God takes the glory in your life, He takes the shame too. If you are taking the shame on your own, it means that you have been taking the glory yourself.

God is not a selfish God Who is only there for you when things are good to receive the glory. He is always there for you in both the shame and the good times. In Isaiah 43:2 God says, "**When you go through deep waters I will be with you. When you go through rivers of difficulty, you will not drown. When you walk through the fire of oppression you will not be burned up; the flames will not consume you**". In verse 3 He says, "**For I am the Lord, your God**". This means that, no matter what, God will never leave you nor forsake you.

Everything God does in your life is for His glory. This means that He can never fail you. As previously mentioned, God is not a selfish God, but He is a jealous God. He wants all the glory to come to Him. He doesn't want to share glory with other gods, or even with you. You need to know God's position in your life and know your position. God wants you to put Him above all things, even above yourself. He wants you to put Him above your career, your money, your business, your family, your house, your car and everything that you have. If you don't, He may take away or remove any of these things to get you to exalt only Him.

This is because He created you mainly to **worship Him** forever. Matthew 6:33 says, "**Seek the Kingdom of God above all else and live righteously, and He will give you everything you need**". God is the only One Who deserves all the glory in all things.

When you give the depression attack to God, He will deliver you from it for His glory.

CHAPTER 10

HE IS A GOD WHO SHOWS OFF!

When God does something, He does it in a way that shows that it was Him Who did it. He does things in a way that doesn't make sense according to human logic. He does things in a way that automatically brings Him glory. When God decides to heal you, He will heal you from a disease or condition that even doctors failed to cure you from.

If God was doing things to please people, He wouldn't do them the same way. Everything God does is for His glory. The moment you hand over any situation to God, the way He handles it is no longer about you, but about Him. The moment you hand over depression to God, the way He gives you victory over it is mainly about Him: it is for His Name to be glorified.

God will show up at just the time when it seems like you have already been defeated and there is no rescue for you. He shows up at the time when it is about to be over for you and gives you **an overwhelming victory**. He creates a new beginning at the point that seems like the end. At the **right time,** God creates a new thing. This is why the Word of God says God is **always** on time, **never** late **nor** early.

CHAPTER 11

WHY DEPRESSION?

When the enemy uses sickness to attack you, even though being sick is physically painful and it does also affect you mentally, there is usually that hope that if you go to the hospital and get treated and take some medication you will be healed. This kind of attack has a known and proven solution, which puts your mind at ease. But depression is different. With depression, the mind is causing the suffering.

When a person is attacked by depression, their strongest organ is the weakest. The mind that normally gives them hope that they will be healed when they are sick, has no hope at all when they are depressed. It seems like they have reached a dead end, and their function system is shuttered. It seems and feels like there is no hope for recovery, because every solution they think of leads them to the same point: a dead end with no solution.

When it comes to depression, the enemy studies the individual's personality in full detail, even the smallest details, which might seem insignificant or irrelevant. The enemy does this to ensure that when he attacks that individual with depression, chances of them surviving the attack are zero. The enemy also observes how the individual handles things in their lives in general. Are they easily angered? Do they have soft hearts? Are they insecure or sensitive people? All those things are part of his study and observation to attack the person.

After such a study, the enemy then executes his attack, which is aimed at killing the person at the end. Remember, the enemy's purpose is to **steal** from you, to **kill** you and to **destroy** you. So, if you are the one he attacks, that is his goal and he has no mercy.

The enemy uses depression as a strong weapon because it attacks the strongest part of a person. The mind is what makes some people wealthy and some poor for the rest of their lives – based on their belief. So, if you think the mind is not that powerful, think about it again. The mind – **your thoughts** – determines your entire life. **It is that powerful**.

When the enemy attacks your mind, your entire body function is affected. This may even affect your health because your mind can't function properly to govern your bodily functions anymore. The funny thing is that depression is the oddest attack in our society. It is not taken seriously, and people make their own assumptions about it, and tend to think they are much stronger than a person who is depressed. In society, a depressed person is the weakest person they have ever seen.

In fact, once people learn about a person being depressed, they have found something very funny to talk about. Funny, right? But the weirdest thing is that the wealthiest people we know or hear about have used the mind to achieve their wealth. While there are billions and billions of people who also have the mind (have the capability) that wealthy people have, those people are still poor. This excludes those who are poor due to very severe circumstances they couldn't prevent or avoid. This is just one example out of many others that shows that **the mind is a strong weapon after all**.

Is the attack of the mind for the weak? It can't be. If it was, the mind would not be what controls the vital functions of the body daily, ensuring that a person functions the way they do. Even though this happens involuntary (subconsciously), the mind is what controls it. The mind would not produce successful people if it was weak, now would it?

If the mind was weak, it would then take something greater and stronger than the mind to produce the best out of people. Even the heart cannot perform all the functions that the mind is responsible for. Another fact is that the heart can be replaced if it does not function properly (if it is impaired), but the mind cannot be replaced. These are just facts that show that the mind is not weak after all.

Once the mind is determined on something, that thing has been achieved already. If you believe that you are a strong, determined and successful person, then you are. If you believe that you conquer anything that comes your way, it won't be easy for you to be convinced otherwise. Your mindset is determined to conquer and overcome in all circumstances. If you have such a mindset, it is not easy for you to be intimidated or to be weak in difficult situations. It will take a well-planned attack of your mind to weaken you and change your belief. This is why the enemy uses depression to attack people.

It is only by God's grace that certain people don't ever experience depression in their lives. It is not that they are stronger than others but that God chose to spare them from it. For those who get to experience it, God knows that through His power (not their own strength) they will overcome it.

People who experience depression can't even explain how they really feel because they are filled with a deep feeling of numbness and defeat, with no hope of recovery. It takes a lot of effort for the enemy to turn a person from being strong to that level of weakness. At first, the person might experience an occurrence once; then it happens again, starting as an irregular pattern. At this point, the person is convinced that they will overcome it, and they are able to ignore it. From there, such an occurrence will start happening repeatedly and it starts to occupy the person's mind (thoughts) day by day, until the person is unable to ignore it.

The enemy's goal is to get the person to a point where it seems like there is no way forward, a point that seems like a dead-end. There are various strategies that the enemy can use to get a person depressed, which were mentioned earlier in this book. For example, a person can be a graduate who is unemployed. First the person can endure unemployment and be able to convince themselves that there are a lot of people going through the same thing (unemployment). But after five, six or seven years of being unemployed, this can start creating a negative mindset in the person. Negative thoughts may start to flood the person's mind.

These thoughts may get the person to make their own conclusions and ask themselves questions like:

- Will I ever get a job?
- Does this mean I will never manage to take care of my own needs, not even once?
- Is God going to give me an opportunity to be employed?
- Does God care about me?
- Is this God's plan for my life?
- Has God forgotten about me?
- Will God answer my prayers?

The answers they usually get from their minds while asking themselves these questions in anger are:

- God doesn't care about me.
- God doesn't love me
- God has forgotten about me
- My life will never move forward; it will be stuck in this position forever.
- I will never achieve anything in life.

All these thoughts are intended to get the person depressed.

CHAPTER 12

WHAT TO DO WHEN YOU GET ANGRY WITH GOD BECAUSE OF YOUR SITUATION?

The hardest thing to do when you are in a situation where you see no solution, where you have no hope anymore, is understanding why God allowed the situation in the first place. If He says He will always protect you, then why did He allow such a situation in your life? You may ask yourself, and even ask God, this question:

- *What did I do for You to punish me this way?*

You may say to God, *"If I have sinned before You, please show me my sin so that I can ask for your forgiveness"* (this is what Job said in Job 7:20*)*. You may even say to God, *"You do not need to punish me this way, it is not necessary"*. You may repeatedly say, *"Please show me my sin that deserves this punishment?"* You may ask these kinds of questions until you get angry with God.

You may start thinking that God doesn't really care about you because if He did He wouldn't have allowed such things to happen to you. You may ask God, *"How is it that you protect me but still allow such a thing to happen to me?"* You may think that, if God really loves you, He would fight for you and save you from such a situation before it can even attack you. You may ask yourself, *"Where is God's love now?"*

These questions may get you angry with God to a point where you feel like it is pointless to pray anymore. This will be because

Oliviah Mona

you feel like God doesn't care about you anymore. You may even feel betrayed by God. You may say to God, *"After I served you so well and was faithful to your instructions, is this how you reward me?"* This may make you angrier with God and make you blame Him for not protecting you.

The battle we are fighting is not against flesh and blood enemies, but is against evil rulers and authorities of the unseen world. It is against mighty powers in this dark world and against evil spirits in the heavenly places (Ephesians 6:12). If it were a physical battle, it would not be so brutal. If it were a physical battle, you wouldn't even get to experience certain attacks that you experience in your life. But this battle is a spiritual battle with the intention to destroy you so that the Will of God is not fulfilled in your life.

The battle is not from God but from ruthless spiritual rulers and authorities from the kingdom of darkness (serving Satan the devil/enemy). These rulers and authorities do not care about your feelings and the impact of their attack on your life. If you were wondering why the battle against you is so brutal, this is why: these evil forces are determined to destroy you at all costs; their goal is to stop you from fulfilling the Will of God in your life. Even if that means they must kill you, they will do it.

So, when you feel so angry with God that you don't even feel like praying anymore, **force yourself to pray**. You may bow down with no words coming out of your mouth because of the heaviness of your heart. While bowing down, you may still be wondering, *"What is God's intention about this situation?"* You may even wonder, *"Is God trying to kill me with this situation?"* But at this very moment, when such thoughts start to saturate your mind, interrupt them by forcing yourself to pray.

Force the first words of prayer out of your mouth, then God will give you strength to continue praying. Once you manage to utter the first few words of prayer, ask God to give you strength to continue praying. He will strengthen you. From there, force yourself to pray without ceasing. **You need to stand and pray!** That is the only way out of that battle. There is no other way out. **Prayer** is the only way you will win the battle.

CHAPTER 13

GOD IS WITH YOU DURING THE SITUATION AND HE WILL GET YOU THROUGH IT

As mentioned previously, God says in Isaiah 43:2-3, **"When you go through deep waters, I will be with you. When you go through rivers of difficulty you will not drown. When you walk through the fire of oppression, you will not be burnt up, the flames will not consume you. For I am the LORD, your God, the Holy One of Israel you, your Saviour"**.

This Word means that, whatever you go through, God is always with you in it. In Joshua 1:9, God says, **"This is my command, be strong and courageous, do not be afraid or discouraged, for the Lord your God is with you wherever you go"**. So, remember this: God is always with you wherever you are and in whatever you go through. He loves you and He will never leave you nor forsake you.

Even if you might not feel it, God is **always** with you. While you might not feel His presence sometimes or most of the time during the situation, He is always by your side. He is fighting the battle for you. He is **faithful**! When you surrender everything unto Him, there is **no way** He will not show up for you. This is because He cannot **fail** His Word. He is **faithful** to His promises as per His Word. If God were to fail to fulfil His Word, He would be failing Himself and that is not the God He is. Since He said in His Word that He will **never** leave you nor forsake you, indeed **He will never leave you** and **He will never forsake you**.

CHAPTER 14

STOP OVER EXPLAINING YOURSELF!

In Hebrews 4:13, the Word of God says "**Nothing in all creation is hidden from God. Everything is naked and exposed before His eyes, and He is the One to Whom you are accountable**". God is the only One you are accountable to.

When a person is going through depression, they are mostly misunderstood. Most of the time, the person's own life does not depress them. They are, in fact, happy and at peace in their lives. But what people say about them makes them depressed. They are constantly trying to figure out why people say wrong and hurtful things about them. This happens when the enemy has decided to attack a person with false accusations or with lies.

One thing about most people, out of many other things, is that they enjoy anything negative, period! If it is a good thing that they hear about a person, it won't interest them that much. However, if they happen to hear something bad, no matter how untrue it may be, they don't even need to verify: they immediately get excited and focus on spreading that gossip about the person. Verification might take the fun out of the lie or whatever it is that was said.

Most people easily believe negative things; this happens effortlessly. This may be due to their own life circumstances so that, when they hear something very bad about another person, something that seems worse than their own circumstances, it makes them feel better about themselves. They get excited about someone else's misery. Are the person's *"said circumstances"* true or not? That doesn't matter.

So, at this point the person being talked about is wondering why people are saying all those things they are saying about them, without even verifying. They wonder why people are so focused on them. They end up feeling like they need to justify themselves. They feel the urge to explain themselves and vindicate themselves from all the lies told about them. Most of the time, the enemy is using **exactly** that to destroy the person by attacking them with lies. The enemy may intentionally make people misunderstand the person to frustrate them.

If the person now tries to explain themselves to clear their names, they realise that, instead of things getting better, they get worse. After clarifying, the person may be called a *liar*. Whatever clarification they give may be classified as a lie. How frustrating is that? The more the person tries to set the record straight, the more what they say is taken out of context, and they become labelled as a *liar*. This is so frustrating! The person's life on its own does not depress them, but lies floating around about them and misunderstandings end up depressing the person.

In such a situation, if you are the affected person, you must understand that people choose to believe what they want to believe. If they did not believe what they heard about you and wanted to verify if it was true, they would have come to you to ask about it, to hear the truth. If they didn't come, it means that they understood and believed what they heard.

Some people might have heard it and dismissed it as a lie without coming to you to verify. Those people chose not to believe the lie. So, whether people believe or do not believe something, that's a choice they make. You can't really change their minds about it, and there's nothing you can do about it. This is not a matter of misunderstanding that maybe you need to clarify. They have already decided to believe what they have heard, so leave it at that. Even if you can try to explain yourself, they won't believe you. So please, as hurtful as it is and as horrible as it feels, don't explain yourself.

You might ask yourself, "What must I do then, since what they are saying about me is not true?" Just to take you to the Word, in Matthew 12:22-32, Jesus the Son of God was said to be getting His power from Satan, the prince of demons. You can just imagine, Jesus, **the Son of God**. But Jesus's response was, "**And if Satan is casting out Satan, he is divided and fighting against himself?**" (You may read all the verses mentioned here to get a full understanding).

What the Pharisees were saying here about Jesus really didn't make sense, like at all. But did it make sense to them? Yes it did, because they were trying to distract Jesus. That was their intention, so that He could not fulfil His purpose.

Did Jesus start feeling miserable about Himself? Did He try to explain Himself? No, He didn't. He knew it would be a waste of time. He said that, if Satan is casting out Satan from people, then he is divided and fighting against himself, which again doesn't make sense.

It really makes no sense most of the time what people think or say about other people, especially when they say negative things. When you think about it, you would wonder, "**Is this how people really think?**" Like, seriously? So, remember this: your battle is for God, not you. In instances when you are misunderstood and lied about, go to God and talk to Him about it. After all, you are accountable to God, not people.

You will realise that, as you pray and no longer explain yourself, God gives you peace and strength to carry on. Some people may realise that your reliance on God is getting stronger, especially if God says to you to fast and pray often. They may start making fun of your prayer life as well, and your growing **trust** in God. This is intended to distract you and make you feel miserable and depressed again.

Listen, you need to break this cycle. **Never stop praying!** Keep asking for strength from God and for His intervention. Pray while they are laughing about your faith; pray while they are laughing about the lies they spread about you. **Pray! Pray! Pray! Never stop praying**. Ask God to vindicate you. Don't try to vindicate yourself.

Remember, this battle is not against those physical people you see who are trying to make your life miserable. It is rather spiritual: a more powerful battle than you think. You need God to fight it for you. Don't lie to yourself: you won't survive. In this battle, spirits that are way older than you are fighting you (they have been there from generation to generation to generation). Ruthless, evil spirits are fighting you (Ephesians 6:12). Please stop trying to clarify your name and **pray**. If you don't need to explain yourself to God, then why are explaining yourself to people? What can they do for you that God cannot do for you?

The one thing you must know and never forget is that this life is mainly about God and you. Yes, you need to live with people, and you need to live in harmony with them. But you don't owe them anything. You don't owe them your life, for that matter. There is nothing they did for you that allows them to have control over your life, while on the other hand you owe God your life entirely. You belong entirely to Him. Remember that and never forget it.

The truth is that the people you are trying to prove yourself to are also trying to prove themselves to other people. It goes on like that from person to person. Some people talk more often about the lies they have heard about you, to try to make themselves feel less miserable about themselves. You have a choice: either you choose a miserable life in which you are always trying to explain yourself to people and always feel miserable afterwards. Or you can choose to surrender to God and never get to explain yourself again. Make a wise choice: choose to surrender to God.

God is all **powerful** and **mighty**. If He didn't want you alive, He would have taken your life a long time ago. For some people, He would have decided that you wouldn't even be born. **But listen, you are here because God wants you here**. He chose to keep you alive, so make sure that you make the best out of the life God gave you.

Whether people talk about you or not, they don't have the power to give you breath, to take that breath, to wake you up in the morning and to preserve your life. They themselves are at **God's mercy** to be alive too. So, what do they have that makes you give them so much power over your life? **What makes you allow them to have control over your life?**

Again, what do you do when people always misunderstand you and make you feel like you need to keep explaining yourself? Here is what you do: **talk to God about it**! He already knows about the situation, but tell Him everything about your situation like He doesn't know. This is not to inform Him but to make yourself feel better. To seek help from God. Don't leave anything out when you tell God about your situation. Tell Him how it makes you feel and how it is affecting your life overall. He is in **charge** of your life. Ask **Him** to **vindicate** you and give you **strength** to overcome the situation. Ask Him to protect you and help you.

If it makes you feel angry, tell God about it. If it makes you want to hurt yourself, tell God about it. If it makes you hate your life because you didn't do anything wrong to deserve it, tell God about it. Tell God everything and ask Him to help you. Ask Him to fight for you and deliver you.

Philippians 4:6 says, "**Don't worry about anything; instead, pray about everything. Tell God what you need and thank Him for all He has done**." This is what you need to do in such a situation. Give it all to God because the battle is not yours, but **God's**! If it is His battle, then why are you trying to fight it yourself? Why are you fighting a battle that doesn't belong to you? Give it all to **God**.

When you go to verse 7 of Philippians Chapter 6, it says, "**Then you will experience God's Peace which exceeds anything you can understand. His Peace will guard your hearts and minds as you live in Christ Jesus**". So, give everything to God and He will give you **His Peace** in return. While facing depression, you need God. He will give you His peace, which will calm you down and give you confidence that God will take care of it. It gives you confidence and assurance that God already took care of the depression.

CHAPTER 15

GOD'S PEACE

The only place you can find peace in such a situation is in God. God Himself is your **Source** of **Peace**. There is no other place where you can find peace except for in Him. Money will not give you peace; people will not give you peace; material things will not give you peace. Nothing can give you peace except for God **Himself**.

As previously mentioned from Philippians 4:7, the Word of God says that, when you have given (surrendered) everything that worries you to God, when you have told Him what you need, and you have thanked Him for all He has done for you, then God will give you His Peace, which exceeds anything you can understand. His Peace will guard your heart and mind as you live in Christ Jesus.

How amazing is that! You give what bothers you to God, and He gives you His Peace in return. It may often seem like, when you have given your life to God, you always face challenges and you keep fighting battles, while those who are not Christians don't face that. But that is not true. People go through so many challenges in their different lives, whether they believe in God or not.

All people fall sick at some point in their lives (whether they are Christians or not). All people lose loved ones at some point in their lives. Some people are abused; some are killed. Good and bad things happen to all people, whether they are Christians or not. However, what is true is that the enemy attacks those who believe in God more than those who don't. This is mainly to destroy the kingdom of God. God's plan for His people is to prosper them and not to harm them, to give them a future and hope. The enemy is fighting exactly that. Furthermore, God promised His people eternal life after death. The enemy is fighting that too. The enemy constantly fights those who believe in God to ensure that no one makes it to eternal life.

In John 14:27, Jesus says, "**I am leaving you with a gift, peace of mind and heart. And the peace I give is a gift the world cannot give. So don't be troubled or afraid.**" This shows that peace of mind and heart only comes from God through Jesus Christ, **the Prince of Peace**. There is nowhere else you can find it. Elsewhere, you might find temporary peace, but the kind of peace which exceeds all understanding and lasts forever can only be found through Jesus Christ. The peace God gives you through Jesus Christ, **the world cannot give to you. Therefore, the world cannot take God's Peace from you**.

CHAPTER 16

IT IS BECAUSE OF WHO YOU BELONG TO THAT YOU ARE ATTACKED

In Isaiah 43:1, God says, "**Listen to the Lord who created you, the one who formed you says, "Do not be afraid, for I have ransomed you. I have called you by name; you are mine.**" In this verse, God is making it clear that you don't belong to anyone else but Him. God ransomed you through the **death** and **resurrection** of **Jesus Christ**. Because you belong to God, your destiny is determined by God.

God knew you before you were born. Every day of your life is recorded in His book; every moment is laid out before a single moment has passed (Psalm 139:16). In Jeremiah 29:11 God says, "**I know the plans I have for you; they are plans for good and not for disaster, to give you a future and a hope**".

It is because you belong to God that the enemy always attacks you; he has no other reason to do so. God destined you for greatness and for an abundant life. The enemy is after that. He is after you because you are a child of God. The greater the attack of the enemy, the greater God's destiny is for your life. This means that if the attack you are experiencing is very severe, God's plans for your life are great. In other words, **you intimidate the enemy**.

The unfortunate part is that you yourself may not physically see the great destiny God gave you, but God does and so does the enemy in spirit. This is where **faith** comes in; you also can see that great destiny, but only through faith, not by sight. This destiny for your life is the reason why the enemy is attacking without even giving you a break.

You might wonder, *"What did I do wrong to attract these numerous attacks from the enemy?"* You didn't do anything wrong. He attacks you mainly because you are a **child of God** and because your destiny might destroy his kingdom.

It is important to note that God didn't say we will not face challenges just because we belong to Him. He didn't say we will never be attacked by the enemy, but He said that He will be with us. He will always fight for us, and He will always give us victory (Isaiah 43:2). This means that God is always with you at every moment of your life, and there is no moment when He is never with you. God is fighting for you, and He will deliver you from the schemes and the attacks of the enemy.

Whatever you go through in life, be it sickness, loss, depression, anxiety, rejection and all other sorts of challenges, God is with you in it. You need to trust Him. When you get tired and weary because the situation is not changing, pray to God. Ask Him to give you strength to stand and overcome. Your victory was already given to you through the death and resurrection of Jesus Christ. Jesus' Blood has redeemed you from any kind of battle or attack that the enemy can bring against you. The Blood of Jesus redeemed you forever. You have already overcome. Overwhelming victory is yours, **in the Name of Jesus Christ**.

You need to pray without ceasing. **No matter what, pray**. When things are good, **pray**. When things are bad, **pray**. When things are ugly, **pray**. When things work against you, **pray**. When people turn against you, **pray**. Always know and never forget that, when things and people turn against you, it doesn't mean that God has turned against you as well. He will never leave you nor forsake you. He will always be with you, and He will always be by your side. **So, keep on praying to God. He is faithful, always**.

In Isaiah 43:4 God says, "**You are precious to me. You are honoured and I love you**". That is all you need: the **unfailing love of God**. When you feel weak, **pray**. Ask God to give you strength to remain **standing**. After every battle, you must remain standing through **Jesus Christ** Who strengthens you.

In Isaiah 43:13 God says, "**From eternity to eternity I am God. No one can snatch anyone out of my hand. No one can undo what I have done**." This is assurance for you that, if your life is in God's hands, no one can snatch it out of His hands. Trust in God wholeheartedly and surrender your life entirely unto Him. He is a **faithful God Who never fails**. He will never ever **fail** you, not even once. He always wins and He has already won the battle for you.

CHAPTER 17

WHAT IT MEANS NOT TO WORRY ABOUT ANYTHING (PHILIPPIANS 4:6)

To remind you again, the Word of God says , "**Don't worry about anything; instead, pray about everything. Tell God what you need and thank Him for all He has done**." (Philippians 4:6) This means that whatever can worry you is worth **praying** about. If being misunderstood by people worries you, then pray about it. If people's lies about you worry you, then pray about it. Whatever can occupy your mind and cause you to worry is worth praying about.

You must remember that God created you. He knows everything about you: your thoughts, worries and so on. He sees everything that happens in your life. God already knows what you feel too weak to tell Him. **He Already Knows**. It is not a new thing to Him. It will never shock Him at all. So, tell Him everything. Don't leave anything out. If you are struggling with anger and you are unable to control your anger, tell God about it. If you are struggling with fear or anxiety, tell God about it. If you are struggling with swearing when angry, tell God about it. Remember, **He Already Knows about it**. Please give it all to God because He cares about you.

Matthew 6:27 says, "**Can all your worries add a single moment to your life?**" Of course not. Not at all. It just robs you of today's joy and peace. It robs you of the life in abundance that Jesus Christ died for you to have. If anything worries you, give it to God. Ask Him to help you and ask Him to give you His Peace for you not to worry about it anymore. Give it all to God.

He cares about you. God will always take care of you, and He will give you His Peace (Philippians 4:7). This doesn't mean you won't have problems, but it means that God will take care of you in the midst of your problems. It means that He will give you His Peace while He fights your battles for you.

The battle doesn't belong to you; it belongs to God. You need to understand this, **always**. Yes, whatever attacks you affects your life, but you don't have the power to fight it by yourself. The enemy aims to steal your joy, your peace, your happiness, your destiny and everything that pertains to you. The enemy doesn't end at stealing, but he also aims to kill and destroy you completely (John 10:10).

This is why the enemy cannot fight you with a battle you can easily overcome. He doesn't come up with a battle that matches your level of strength, otherwise he will never achieve his goal. The enemy attacks you, intending that in the end you will be destroyed. This is why you **need God**. God is Spirit, the enemy is spirit, while you are human (physical/flesh). You are not weak, but God is strong enough to defeat Satan for you. Only God can defeat the enemy.

In 2 Chronicles 20:15, the Word of God says, "**Do not be afraid! Don't be discouraged by this mighty army, for the battle is not yours, but God's**". Verse 17 says, "**You will not even need to fight. Take your positions; then stand still and watch the Lord's victory**." God already gave you victory. Again, give the battle entirely to God, **pray without ceasing**. No one can stand against you when God is on your side.

CHAPTER 18

HOW TO PRAY WITHOUT CEASING
(1 THESSALONIANS 5:17)

In Jeremiah 1:19 God says, "**They will fight you, but they will fail. For I am with you, and I will take care of you. I the Lord have spoken**." What does the Word mean here? It means that, because you belong to God and have given your life to Him, the enemy will fight you, but he will always **fail**. In fact, the enemy will fight you more because you belong to the kingdom of God. But if you pray without stopping, you will always have God's covering upon your life. God will **make sure** the enemy always fails.

If the enemy fights you with depression, God will **ensure** that you overcome it. But you should pray **without ceasing** (1 Thessalonians 5:17). Pray every day. Trust God with all your heart. If you are not consistent in your prayer, you are allowing the enemy to have a free pass into your life. Remember, the enemy will never stop fighting you. He is fighting you every day and night.

Satan will never stop fighting you just because you are tired or because you have won the last battle he had against you. Satan will keep coming for you, so you need to be geared up through prayer. You need to be armed with **the Word of God** and **prayer**, to overcome the enemy's strategies and battles against you. You need to pray strongly to overcome, period.

CHAPTER 19

DECLARE THE WORD OF GOD UPON YOUR LIFE EVERY DAY

Hebrews 4:12 says, "**For the Word of God is alive and powerful. It is sharper than the sharpest two-edged sword, cutting between soul and spirit, between joint and marrow. It exposes our innermost thoughts and desires**". The Word of God is God Himself. So, when you speak God's Word over your life, you are speaking God Himself.

When you speak God's Word over anxiety, stress, depression, anger, heartbreak, betrayal, sickness, rejection, failure, loss and many other difficult situations, there is no way God cannot act. God is faithful to His promises, which are His Word. This is why in Isaiah 55:11 God says, "**He sends His Word, and it always produces fruit. It accomplishes all He wants it to, and it prospers everywhere He sends it**." So, there is no way you can declare God's Word continuously and nothing happens. If you declare God's Word in **faith**, it will bring about results.

God acts in response to His Word. In Joshua 1:8, God says, "**Study this book of instruction continually. Meditate on it day and night so you will be sure to obey everything written in it. Only then will you prosper and succeed in all you do.**" This is a clear instruction; it can't get clearer than this. God commands us to read His Word continually, for us to be able to obey His instructions, and to speak His Word boldly in our lives without fear and without hesitation.

Speaking the Word of God in your life is not a once-off thing or an occasional occurrence; it is a lifestyle. You need to declare

God's Word daily. This should be how you live your life; through every Word that God has spoken. Even when a situation is getting worse in your life, declare **His Word** more. When you get more depressed, declare and believe God's Word more. Never stop declaring God's Word and praying because things are getting worse. The worse they get, the more you should stand by God's Word. Declare it, pray and you will overcome.

Even when it feels like nothing has changed for a very long time, keep declaring the Word of God. It is prevailing. God is working things out for your good. You may not see the change while you are declaring the Word of God daily, but believe that He is working things out for your good, because He is. As per Isaiah 55:11, **God's Word** always works. God's Word never fails; it will never start failing with you. **There is no way!** His Word always manifests.

God's plans for you are intended to prosper you. They are not intended to harm you. His plans are intended to give you a future and hope. **God is not a man that He can lie. He is not human that He can change His mind**. He stands by His Word. The one thing you must know about God and never forget is that **God Never Fails. He has never failed before; He will never fail, ever**.

Yes, it feels like things are not changing as you keep on praying. As you keep on declaring God's Word, it feels like things remain the same or get worse. Yes, it feels like God is not there with you, but know this: **God is always there for you. He is always with you**. As you pray, God is fighting battles for you that you do not see. As you keep on praying, God is destroying and cancelling plans that were meant to destroy you.

Physically, you may get tired when you keep on praying to God about the same thing and it doesn't change. You may get very discouraged and end up wanting to give up. But try your level best not to give up. **Keep on praying**. When you get tired, ask God for strength to keep standing firm in prayer.

The enemy's intention is to get you tired so that you give up. Don't give the enemy the satisfaction. Even when it gets worse and worse, know this: **Your God Never Fails**. Even when things get worse, to a point where it seems like everyone is against you, where it seems like everyone is laughing at you, laughing about your situation, **keep on praying**. God already gave you victory.

CHAPTER 20

BE THANKFUL IN ALL CIRCUMSTANCES (1 THESSALONIANS 5:18)

God is aware that we will go through challenges. He is aware that our lives have good times and bad times. Life is structured that way and everyone goes through different stages of life, facing the good and the bad at such times. But the Word of God says, "**Be thankful in all circumstances for this is God's Will for you in Christ Jesus**" (1 Thessalonians 5:18).

This means that there is **always** something to be thankful for, even during the bad times. You woke up today, you are alive: be thankful. You are healthy and not sick: be thankful. Your family is safe: be thankful. You still have a job: be thankful. You have a home and food to eat: be thankful. Your spouse and children are safe: be thankful. You can still eat by yourself, you can see, touch, talk, walk, hear: **be thankful**. Always be thankful in all circumstances, whether good or bad.

Be thankful for the unfailing love of God. The love of God always provides for you. You cannot have **nothing** to be thankful for if God is in your life. If you can just observe your life closely every day, you will see how great God is. You will see that He does a lot of good things for you. You can't even count the good things God does for you.

God saves you from accidents daily (some near accidents you witness, and some you don't). He saves you from sicknesses and diseases, some of which He heals you from and some He prevents from attacking you altogether. There is **no way** you can have God and have nothing to be grateful for. This is why the enemy keeps distracting you with negativity and lies: to stop you from realising how great God is. The enemy wants to steal the joy of seeing the greatness of God in your life. God is **always great**!

When the enemy attacks your mind with depression, it is not because you are weak; it is because you are strong in God. It is because if the enemy doesn't distract your mind, you will accomplish the **great** things God destined your life for. Unfortunately, the enemy knows what God deposited in you, which you can't see in the physical. This is why he fights you until he defeats you and takes it. This can take years, but he is determined to fight you until he gets what he wants. Of course, if you are fighting this battle by yourself against Satan, you will have lost before you even start.

Don't allow the enemy to win; give the battle entirely to **God**. If the enemy constantly fights you, either with different attacks or he holds on to one attack with which he wants to destroy you, then what he is fighting you for is worth it. He sees something great that distracts him and he can't even ignore it. So, stand firm and overcome him. Stand with faith in **prayer**, and let God protect what is rightfully yours.

CHAPTER 21

YOUR COMMITMENT TO GOD DEPENDS ON HOW DESPERATE YOU ARE FOR HIM

The amount of time you spend with God depends on how desperate you are for His presence. Yes, it depends on how desperate you are for His intervention in your life. If you have options other than God, it makes sense to just relax and go to God occasionally, whenever you feel like you need Him. If you have backup and other plans that work for you, then you may occasionally seek to be in God's presence.

But, if God is your only option in life, you will be committed to Him. If your life depends only on God, your commitment to Him will show. You won't approach Him with a mindset of Him being an option for you. Instead, you will approach Him in a manner that shows your full dependence on Him. The extent to which you are committed to God is based on how dependent you are on Him. Your commitment to Him shows that nothing makes sense without God.

In 2 Corinthians 1:9, Paul says, **"we stopped relying on ourselves, and learned to rely only on God, who raises the dead"**. In this verse, complete dependence on God is demonstrated. This is where you say, no matter what, you put all your trust in God. When you read verse 8 of the same chapter, Paul mentions that they went through trouble beyond their ability to endure. They were overwhelmed by trouble that they didn't even expect to live through, but expected to die from. When they learned to rely only on God, God rescued them.

The amount of time you spend with God depends on how much you rely on Him. If you fully depend on God, your prayer life will show. You cannot forget to pray if you cannot live without God; there is just no way. If you still care a lot about what people say or think, what their opinions are about your life in Christ, then you might still have other options you depend on. You do not fully depend on God yet. Because, if you get to a state where God is everything to you, it won't matter what people think or say, you will make sure that you are always in God's presence. You will be aware that you can't survive without God. You can't survive without being in His presence. It really does matter Who God is to you. That determines your level of commitment to Him.

God will only manifest in your life if you fully depend on Him. He will reveal Himself in your life if He is in full control of it. God is always available to help us, but the question is, are we always available to Him to receive His help? **Faith,** according to Hebrews 11:1, is defined as "**the confidence that what we hope for will actually happen; it gives us assurance about things we cannot see**".

It is true that we do not see what God is doing when we pray. We cannot see what our prayer is doing to the situation. As a result, when things don't seem to be changing while we pray, we get discouraged and think that our prayer is not working. We stop praying and we give up, but prayer **always** works. There is no way you can pray and nothing happens in the spiritual realm. Only God sees what your prayer is doing in your situation but, because you trust God, you must know that your prayer is working. This is what **faith** is all about. It is about trusting in God always, even if you don't see what He is doing. It is about believing God based on His Word. It is about fully believing that God will do what He said He will do for you.

As you are praying and nothing seems to be changing or nothing seems to be happening, occupy your mind with the Word of God. Say to yourself, "**I know God will never fail me**". Say "**I know God will never leave me nor forsake me**". Say to yourself, "**God's plans for my life are for my good and not for disaster. To give me a future and a hope**." Speak God's Word every day. Occupy your mind with God's Word. Trust and know that God is working things out for your good.

It is not easy to stay strong at this point but hold on, stand firm and believe God. Believe God beyond your reality (what you see). Always know that God never fails and He will never fail you. Depression is not something that you see, but it is what you feel. Someone cannot know that you are depressed unless you say it. Faith is also not something you can see, but it is what you believe in. It is knowing in your heart that things are working out for your good. Both the depression and your faith that others can't see, God can see, and He is the only One you need to look up to for help. In the Word of God, especially in the book of Matthew, many people were healed because of their faith. They believed that they were healed, and they were healed.

God always has your best interests at heart; He has the best plans for your life. Spend your time close to Him daily, and seek His presence always. Fight to stay in God's presence because it is where you belong. **Prioritising God requires discipline**. Like when you dedicate time to study or work, you also need to dedicate time for God and be disciplined to spend that time with Him. Sometimes, you feel like studying or working; sometimes you don't. But whether you feel like it or not, you need to do these things. It is the same with reading the Word of God and praying. Whether you feel like praying or not, you need to ensure that you always pray on time and are punctual about it.

Most of the time we make excuses when we must pray and we expect God to understand our excuses, but we still expect Him to meet our needs. We still expect Him to bless us and protect us every day, which is not how it works. Like work, you cannot be paid by a company you do not work for. Like with money, you cannot withdraw from a bank you do not deposit money into. Like at school, you cannot pass an exam or test you did not study for. You cannot expect God to always protect you and be there for you when you do not even prioritise Him in your life.

When it comes to God, we often want to take advantage. We think that because He loves us He will do everything for us without any effort from our end. That is not how faith works. Faith requires work too. Like everything that is important in your life, you need to ensure that you dedicate time to read your bible and pray. To avoid being late for work or school, you set an alarm to wake up on time and to arrive on time. It is the same principle for prayer: you need to set an alarm to pray on time if you are struggling to keep your prayer time on your own. Make no excuses!

Sometimes, you will feel lazy to pray but you should force yourself to pray because prayer is always for your benefit. The Word of God in 1 Thessalonians 5:17 says, "**Pray Without Ceasing**". This means that **prayer** is a lifetime commitment. You don't pray today, see results and then stop praying. You pray every day for the rest of your life. The enemy doesn't attack you once and then he leaves you alone. He attacks you every day. So, you need to make up your mind and choose to stand your ground firmly every day through prayer. Stand strongly and overcome all the strategies of the enemy through your faith in prayer. This is a choice you make in life: you can either be the enemy's object for mockery, or you can live a victorious life through **Christ**

Jesus Who strengthens you. In life, you can either choose to live a prayerless, defeated life or you can choose to live a victorious prayerful life. Choose wisely: choose a victorious prayerful life.

Everyone knows that when you love someone you want to spend most of your time with them. It can be your parents, your wife, your husband, your children or your friends. You don't avail yourself for everyone at any time, but you make time for those you love. It is the same approach with God. If you love God, you spend most of your time with Him. You make time for Him every day and prioritise His time.

How do you spend time with God? By reading His Word and through prayer. Most people treat God as an option; they only go to God when they need help. They want to get close to Him only when they are troubled or in trouble, but, once He delivers them, they want to go back and live their lives the way they want. This way faith will not work for you.

It is true that God is life, and that we can't live without Him, but even if it is so, Him being a merciful Father He still gives us a choice to choose to either live for Him or not to live for Him. Depending on God is not an option; it is the only way of life. But God still allows you to choose whether you want to depend on Him or not. God will not force you to depend on Him or to prioritise Him.

You need to make a choice that, no matter what, you will prioritise God in your life. This is not just praying in the morning when you wake up and at night before you sleep. You need to make time during the day, read a verse, two verses or a chapter and pray. You can pray at home, in your car, during your lunch break, in the bathroom at work or at school, or even pray within your heart if you can't excuse yourself from other people at the time you want to pray. Don't allow yourself to be silent throughout the day; talk to God. Pray several times during the day, even if it is not long prayers. Giving thanks to God is also a prayer.

You also need to set certain days to fast and pray. A lot of people think that you only fast when you face challenges in your life, so as to overcome them. Other than that, they don't fast. This journey of faith will not work for you if walk in it like that. You fast to get closer to God and to get to know Him better. You learn more about God when you read His Word and pray without distractions. When you fast and pray, God reveals to you truths about Himself that you didn't know. He reveals truths about your life and your destiny that you didn't know. God further gives you guidance and strength to stand firm and overcome this challenging life.

In Psalms 32:8, God says, "**I will guide you along the best pathway for your life**". You will not understand God's guidance if you do not pray. You might miss the best pathway for your life that God has for you because you are not living under His guidance. Prioritise God in your life and you will never regret it.

CHAPTER 22

READING THE WORD OF GOD

The Word of God is a sword of the Spirit. It reveals God's promises and truths concerning our lives. If you are lazy to read the Word of God, you are most likely to pray based on your emotions. This is spiritually dangerous. Praying based on how you feel determines what you will say to God in your prayer. If you pray while angry, most likely you will end up angry with God while you pray, which is not an effective way to pray.

When you are depressed, you are filled with a lot of draining emotions. Those emotions may include discouragement, anxiety, anger, hopelessness, fear, feeling betrayed, worry and a lot of other negative emotions. If you pray in this state, you might end up blaming God for allowing the situation that made you depressed. You may end up feeling betrayed by God. You may get angry with God because you may feel like He didn't protect you.

This is what happens when you pray based on how you feel and not based on the Word of God. This kind of prayer again is not effective. God wants us to pray and live based on the truth that is found in His Word, not based on our emotions. The Word of God is the truth. You need to live, pray and trust in God based on it. Reading the Word of God is vital because it tells you God's plans and thoughts about your life. It reveals God's promises to you and you get to know God better. You learn from the Word of God that He is the One Who fights all battles for you. You only need to trust Him (2 Chronicles 20:15).

God's Word also reveals that in this journey of faith we will face many battles but, as He promised in His Word, He will never leave nor forsake us. In Exodus 14:14, the Word of God says, **"The Lord Himself will fight for you, just stay calm"**. This verse reveals that God is in charge, and He will take care of you. When you read the Word of God, you pray based on it. A prayer without the Word of God is an empty prayer. God is faithful to His promises. When you pray based on His promises, He will fulfil them through your faith. You need to pray based on what God has said, not based on the situation you are facing. When you pray based on Who God is, you will see Him manifest in your life.

CHAPTER 23

HOW TO PRAY WHEN YOU DON'T HAVE STRENGTH TO PRAY

Prayer is not as easy as it sounds. It sounds easy but when you should pray every day, you realise that it is not that easy. This is because life is full of unexpected events that we face in our daily lives. Things we least expect to happen, happen to us. This affects us and, as people are different, we respond in different ways to situations we face.

Some people might react positively to a certain negative occurrence but in other occurrences they might break down to the point of being depressed. That is the unfortunate part of life. Different things happen and we need to be able to deal with them and overcome the impact they have on our lives.

Something very bad can happen to a person, to the point where they even question if prayer works, where the person even questions God. The person may not necessarily question God's existence because they know that God exists, but they may question His intentions about them. They may question whether God's plans for their lives are really for their good. They may question whether He is there for them as He says He is.

At such times, it is very hard to pray. You may feel like there is no point in praying because things will happen the way that they want to happen anyway. At some point, you may even feel like God is the One allowing all the bad things to happen to you, like it is part of His plan for your life.

It is very difficult to pray when you are at this point in life. You may be feeling like God is against you. That is how the enemy wants you to feel, to discourage you from praying. The moment you start questioning God and stop praying, the enemy knows that he gets full access to you. Not only will the enemy steal from you once he has access to you, but he will also destroy you. Remember, the enemy stops at nothing to destroy the Kingdom of God, or rather anyone who is part of the kingdom of God.

So, when you are at the weakest point in your life, where you even start to question God's intentions about your life, stop such evil thoughts by asking God to help you overcome them. Ask God to give you strength to pray so that you can overcome all the strategies of the enemy. God can never contradict His Word. He will do what He said He will do. Nothing can make Him change His mind. He is **faithful** to His Word, no matter what. This is why any time that negative thoughts start to invade your mind, **you need to pray your way out of them and into the presence of God**. Remember, **God never fails,** and **He will never fail you, no matter what.**

Lack of prayer is also an attack from the devil. The devil knows that, when you pray consistently, nothing can stop you from receiving what God has already given to you. You will have an endless access to overflowing promises of God. This is why the enemy does everything in his power to make you weak, powerless and prayerless. This is so that he can steal what God has given you. But don't allow him to do so, for greater is God Who is on your side than the devil in this world.

Pray depressed, pray hurt, pray worried, pray heartbroken, pray disappointed. Pray! Pray! Pray! Whatever you do, never stop praying. Again, Hebrews 11:1 says, "**Faith is the confidence that what we hope for will actually happen; it gives us assurance about things we cannot see.**" So, be encouraged to pray even if you don't see the results immediately. Just keep on praying. No matter what, never stop praying because God hears your prayer every time you pray, and He has already answered your prayers.

He has already done for you exceedingly, abundantly, above all that you have asked or thought, according to His power that is at work in you (Ephesians 3:20). **Trust God and His process. Wait for Him in prayer.** He has already come through for you. In Isaiah 64:4, the Word of God says, "**For since the world began, no ear has heard, no eye has seen a God like Him Who works for those who wait for Him**". Trust God's process and wait for Him in prayer.

For a long time, you may be praying for something and nothing changes, or it may get worse as you pray. Keep on praying, wait for God in prayer. God says in Isaiah 60:22, "**At the right time, I the Lord, will make it happen**". If you have not seen the results of what you are praying for yet, wait in prayer. Praise and worship the Almighty God while things get ugly, while they look like they will never change. God works best in such situations. It is His character to bring to life things that seem dead. God never fails. So, pray. God hears you and He has **already** given you victory. **Amen!**

HOW TO WAIT ON THE LORD

The truth is that answers to our prayers don't always manifest immediately. Sometimes they do, but most of the time they don't. There is usually a period during which you wait for the results of what you prayed for to show. How do you wait in the Lord? You Praise and worship God as you wait. You give thanks to God as you wait. The situation itself might not be resolved yet, but there are a lot of good things God has done for you that you need to be thankful for. Well, the **primary** reason why God created us (people) was to worship Him and that is what you do.

In Jeremiah 32:39, God says, "**I will give them one heart and one purpose, to worship me forever, for their own good and for the good of all their descendants**". Worshipping God is the purpose we were created for. Everything else He gives to us out of His Grace. It is not that God didn't hear your prayer when you don't see the results yet: the right time is coming. As you wait for God's right time, worship Him on your way to victory. Worship God every single day.

God is aware of what you are going through. He hears what they are saying about you. He heard what they said about you in your absence. He is aware of all the pain and tears it has cost you. But God's focus is not on the people hurting you. His focus is on you. What are you saying about Him during all that? Do you still declare that He is the **Alpha and Omega** of your life? Do you still declare that He has won the victory for you?

Do you still say that **His thoughts towards you are of peace and not of evil, to give you a future and hope?** What exactly are you saying about God during those painful times? This is what is important. Do you still give Him all the glory that is due to Him while depressed? Do you still declare that **He is the Almighty God** during that stressful situation?

Where is your **focus** during the time when you are tested? Does your situation change Who God is to you or do you still declare that **there is nothing that God cannot do**? There is nothing that God cannot change. What are you saying to God when things get ugly?

Your focus should always be on glorifying God, no matter what. That is the purpose God created you for. If you can't find a reason to worship God, worship Him because He is God. That is the reason you worship Him. Yes, He will give you every good thing that He wants you to have, but that is out of His Grace and Mercy. You don't worship God because of the things He has given you but because of Who He is. He blesses you because He promised to bless you in His Word. He said you will be blessed going out and blessed coming in.

In Daniel 3:16-18, Shadreck, Meshack and Abednego said to King Nebuchadnezzar, **"We do not need to defend ourselves before you. If we are thrown into the blazing furnace, the God whom we serve is able to save us. He will rescue us from your power, your majesty. But even if He doesn't, we want to make it clear to you your majesty, that we will never serve your gods or worship the gold statue you have set up."**

These verses are a perfect demonstration of trusting God. Especially in verse 18, Shadreck, Meshack and Abednego were determined that, even if God didn't save them from the fire, they would never serve the king's gods or worship his gold statue.

When they said "**even if He doesn't**" it showed that they were fully aware that God may choose not to save them from the fire, but that wouldn't make Him less of God to them or less faithful to His Word.

God's thoughts and His ways are known only by God Himself. He acts and responds differently from the way we think or expect Him to act. So, it is not what He does for us that makes Him great; it is Who He is that makes Him great. Whether He heals you from a disease or not, He is still God. Whether He changes the situation or not, He is still God. **Bear in mind that His thoughts towards you are of peace and not of evil, to give you a future and hope**. No matter what, His Will for your life will prevail. The best thing you can do is to worship Him, give Him thanks in all circumstances because that is His Will for your life in Christ Jesus (1 Thessalonians 5:18).

Worrying about how God will change your situation or how He will respond doesn't help. You need to focus on your part, and He will do the rest. Your part is to trust Him and to give Him all the glory that is due to Him every single day of your life.

If He didn't need any advice when He was creating the heavens and the earth, which are still standing even today, what makes you think He can't change your situation? Can you really guide God on how to respond to your situation or how to deal with it? No, that part is for Him alone.

If God created a human being, if He decided on every feature He wanted a human body to have, and then He brought the human to life – if God sustains a human being every day – what makes you think that He can't handle your situation? Can you help Him fight your battle? Can your worry make God win the battle for you?

Just think about it for a moment. We are not talking about any other god. We are talking about the **Almighty God Who created the heavens and the earth**. How He created them is still a mystery even today. Your mind can't even begin to comprehend how God created everything, including how He created you. That should give you an indication that He is the **Almighty God**. Really, you can't help Him with anything. Even your worry doesn't help Him or you in any way. God can do anything He wants at any time.

God can do whatever He wants whenever He wants to. He can make time stop, the night stand still, the sun not go down. If God wants to, He can take the very life you are stressing about. You are only alive because He chooses to keep you alive. Be thankful for that. It is really a privilege and an honour for our great God to be so loving, so caring, so compassionate and so merciful towards us. It is through His Grace that He does everything He does for us. We cannot even comprehend His greatness.

So, when you start worrying about things not changing in your life, when you worry about things getting worse when you pray about them, remember the God you are praying to and give Him all the glory. That is the least you can do. You can't make God act faster or slower. You can't make God act in a certain way towards a certain situation. **Yours is to focus on the greatness of God and worship Him every single day of your life**. **That is the only way you can wait on God**. Always focus on God and nothing else. Even if God responds in a way that you didn't expect, it is for your good. Don't lose focus. Focus on Who He is and give Him glory.

That way, He will do for you what no ear has heard, and no eye has seen. He will do exceedingly, abundantly, above all you might ask or think, according to His power that is at work in you.

CHAPTER 25

NO EAR HAS HEARD, NO EYE HAS SEEN WHAT GOD WILL DO FOR YOU (ISAIAH 64:4)

In Isaiah 64:4, the Word of God says, "**For since the world began, no ear has heard, no eye has seen, a God like You, who works for those who wait for Him**". The truth remains: **God works things out for our good and He never fails, no matter what.** However, it is important to take note that, even if God works things out, the process of waiting is one we cannot bypass, fast track or escape. We need to wait patiently for His appointed time. **The waiting time is the secret. How you wait determines whether you will make it to God's appointed time or not.**

In the previous chapter, there is a full description of how we wait on the Lord, which is by worshipping Him. As a reminder, you **never** stop praying while you are waiting. Your part is to trust God and have faith in Him. Faith is built by reading the Word of God and by praying without ceasing. If you don't read the Word of God, if you don't pray, you might get tired and give up before you receive God's deliverance for your life.

Since this book is about depression, take note that the devil will keep fighting you and he will stop at nothing until he kills you with that depression. You need to fight back through prayer, and by declaring the Word of God in your life daily. That is how you fight every day. When you get tired or discouraged from praying, ask God to give you strength to carry on praying and reading His Word. Your fight is through your faith in God by prayer. Then God does the rest. God defeats the enemy, and He sets you free completely from the schemes of the enemy. Take note of this: you need to pray, no matter what. **Never stop praying**. Pray to be able to pray. Pray to stand to pray. Always Pray!

That is what you need to do. You cannot stand without prayer. You cannot stand without reading and declaring the Word of God. There is nothing God cannot do for you, but you will not get it without a fight through your faith. **Pray your way out of depression. Pray your way out of anxiety. Pray your way out of failure and rejection. Pray your way out of sickness and disease. Pray your way out of shame and disgrace. Pray, and God will deliver you**.

As you grow in faith through the time you spend with God, God is pleased with you. **Fix your focus on God and you will see what He will do for you**. What God will do for you, even you yourself you cannot think of or imagine. **Trust God and fight to stay in His presence**. He will do things for you that you will not even be able to comprehend. Spend time with God daily and watch Him take you out of that impossible-looking situation, into the destiny He gave you. **Deliverance doesn't come without faith**. Faith is built in prayer, and through reading and speaking the Word of God. What God will do for you, no ear has heard and no eye has seen. Brace yourself: God is about to do a new thing in your life.

CHAPTER 26

FOCUSING ON GOD

It is much easier to focus on God when you are okay and everything seems to be going well in your life – when nothing is troubling you. It is so much easier to focus on God in this state and to make time for Him because you feel favoured by God. But once you have a challenge or certain challenges that torment you and seem not to go away, no matter what you do – even when you fast and pray, they seem not to be shaken and maybe even become worse – then in this state it is not as easy to focus on God.

In this state you may ask yourself a lot of questions, especially if certain challenges have been tormenting you for a long time. You may ask yourself, *"Why is God allowing this to happen to me?"* or, *"What have I done to God to deserve all this?"* It is not very easy to shift from such thoughts and from what is happening to focus on God. You need divine intervention from God to get the strength to shift from such thoughts into His presence. You need His Word to interrupt those negative thoughts and to remind you of Who God is. You need strength from God to look only unto Him, even when all things around you are falling apart.

Focusing on God no matter what requires a certain level of stubbornness. At this level, no matter what happens you stubbornly believe in God's Word, and you believe that God will keep His promises concerning your life. You need to be stubborn in faith to survive this wicked world. You need to be determined that, no matter what, you trust God.

Oliviah Mona

It is not easy to stay focused on God when things just keep getting worse. Things getting worse is a sign that the enemy is fighting you back. Your prayer has an impact on his kingdom. Yes, it is difficult to believe that God will see you through when things keep falling apart. When you keep fasting and praying but it seems like God is not paying attention to your prayer. But God has already heard your prayer, and He has already answered your prayer, although the enemy makes you think that nothing is happening or nothing is changing.

You might end up feeling like God is allowing all those bad things to happen to you. You might end up feeling like God is punishing you for something, although you don't even know what you did wrong. You might end up wondering, *"Does God love me as He says He does?"* You might wonder, *"How does God feel, seeing me suffer like this every day?"* *"Does it make Him happy?"* *"When is He going to show up for me as He promised?"* *"How does He let such things to happen? Really, how?"* You may often wonder about such things and end up discouraged in your prayer life and in life in general.

The more you pray, the worse things often become. This is discouraging, but it shows that your prayer is working. Don't stop praying until you win. This shows that the enemy feels the impact of your prayer and he is fighting back. Even though you can't see the spiritual realm, your prayer is always working. So, when God says to you to fast and pray for a certain period, do it. It is worth it.

Don't give up. Whatever the enemy planned against you will never prevail. If you get weak, ask God for strength to keep praying without ceasing. Focus on God and you will overcome. Whether things get better or worse, stubbornly believe that God has already given you victory. Jesus Christ died for you to be set free, and you are free indeed. Through His death, Jesus disarmed all spiritual rulers and authorities, and nothing and no one can stand against you and prosper. **There is no way that can happen!** Trust God with all your heart; He has already given you victory.

CHAPTER 27

SURRENDER THE SITUATION TO GOD

It is not easy to just ignore a situation that drains and hurts you. You may spend all your energy and time trying to solve the situation at hand. During this time, you might be becoming more drained and hurt, and could even feel hopeless at some point. Often, when you ask people for advice about the situation you are facing, because they have never experienced it themselves or they might have experienced it but it impacted them differently from you, they might say, "**Just ignore it**". They might tell you, "**Don't think about it**". You will wonder, "If it was that easy to not think about it, I would have just done that in the first place. I would not be troubled by the situation in this manner in the first place."

Sometimes, you might end up mad at those who advise you because you feel like they are taking your situation lightly. The truth is that they have never experienced that situation themselves or, if they have experienced it, it did not affect them in the same way as it is affecting you. They don't know how you feel. Some might not have a point of reference for it (those who have not faced such a challenge in their lives), which is why their advice may sound like they think you are weak or that your situation is not as bad as you think it is. It might seem like you are overreacting to the situation. You may feel like they don't care as much as you thought they would.

You may get frustrated because of this. But the truth is that the people from whom you are asking advice are not wrong but they really can't relate to your situation. This might seem like they don't care about you, but they do. It is just that they are not the right people to help you in such a situation. Some people on the other hand might be enjoying that you are going through what you are going through and could even make fun of your situation and criticise you while you are getting hurt. But some people might really not know how to help you.

The only One Who can relate to your situation, comfort you and strengthen you in it is **God Himself**. God created you; He knows everything that will happen in your life before it even happens. Every detail of your life He knows, including the very situation you are going through. He sees all your tears and only **He** knows your story. Run to Him and surrender everything unto Him.

In all difficult situations of our lives, God is there with us. The best thing you can do for yourself is to surrender everything to God. Surrender the pain you feel unto Him. Tell God everything as if He didn't see it as it happened. Vent it all to God so that it can be lifted from your heart into **His Hands**. God will never betray you; He will never make fun of you; He will never criticise you or make you feel like you are weak for not overcoming the situation. After all, He is the reason that you are still alive, still standing. God cares about you, and He wants you to live.

God will help you throughout the situation. He will give you **His Peace and joy** while He is fighting for you. Sometimes, the situation might even be getting worse, but He will give you peace in the midst of it. He will give you the kind of joy you can't even explain.

When you give the situation to God, He gives you His Peace in return. God gives you rest while He fights for you. Whether the storm is still there or not, you will be experiencing His Peace. Whether the situation is getting better or worse, you will be experiencing His Peace, which exceeds your understanding, peace you can't even explain. So, whatever worries you qualifies to be prayed for (Philippians 4:6). Whatever distracts your focus in God deserves to be taken to God's throne. In return, God will give you His Peace.

The challenge is that every time we pray we expect God to fix the situation immediately. But that is not how God works most of the time. God wants us to rejoice and have peace during the situation, trusting that He is taking care of everything. This is what builds our faith in Christ Jesus. When God is involved, peace and joy don't come after the battle; they come during the battle. Rest comes during the battle. This is where our faith grows.

You have to say, "**I am in this with God, the Creator of the heavens, the earth and everything in them**". You shall always rejoice and be glad in the presence of the Lord because there is no way you can lose with Him on your side. Stand, have faith, persevere, be patient and overcome. This is how you win in this journey of faith. This is how you conquer in this walk with Jesus. Surrender it all to God and He shall give you peace, joy and rest in Christ. Through Jesus, you have already won every battle.

CHAPTER 28

DANCING DURING THE STORM

Storms are intended to distract you from your focus on Jesus Christ and the abundant life He made available to you through His death and His resurrection. Overthinking about the storm (the situation) only makes it look worse and too big for you. This will drain your energy and shift your faith in God and in the Lord Jesus Christ, which is the enemy's intention.

The question now is, "**Why is God allowing storms in our lives?**" Why doesn't He protect us from them, so that they never get to happen? Well, there is a reason for the storms. There is a reason why the journey with God is called "**A Walk of Faith**". Without the storms, there is no patience, no endurance, no perseverance and there is no faith (trusting that God is working things out for your good without seeing what He is doing). If your faith is not tested, it cannot be proven. Hence God allows the storms to happen.

Something cannot be classified as a storm if it is in your ability to overcome it. The storm is meant to test your faith in God. This means that only God can rescue you from it. A storm requires you to fully rely on God. The reality is that life is **spiritual**, and there is war between the Kingdom of God and the kingdom of darkness (the kingdom of Satan). So, whether we like it or not, Satan, the devil, will bring those storms to destroy us.

However, God builds our **faith** during those storms. The faith God builds in us leads to our **deliverance**. In other words, your deliverance from storms is dependent on your faith in God. For example, if God asks you to fast and pray for a certain period or according to a certain pattern during a storm or even outside of a storm, **do it in faith**. Know that it is all for your good. If you still care about what people think about your fasting or care about them criticising you about it or making fun of it, you will never get delivered.

The storm is meant to keep your focus in Jesus Christ, no matter what. You need to be obedient to be delivered and overcome. In 2 Corinthians 1:9, Paul says, "**We stopped relying on ourselves and learned to rely only on God who raises the dead**". Verse 10 of the same chapter says, "**And He did rescue us from mortal danger, and He will rescue us again. We have placed our confidence in Him, and He will continue to rescue us**." It is only when you fully rely on God that you get delivered.

Once you have fixed your focus on Jesus Christ, you will experience joy and peace during the storm. You will rejoice and dance in His presence while the storm is getting better or worse. It doesn't matter the state of the storm. What matters is that God will give you joy and peace in the midst of it. You will dance because of the goodness of God and His love that never fails you.

CHAPTER 29

GOD WILL ONCE AGAIN FILL YOUR MOUTH WITH LAUGHTER AND YOUR LIPS WITH SHOUTS OF JOY

In Job 8:21 the Word of God says, "**He will once again fill your mouth with laughter and your lips with shouts of joy**". This is an assurance that, after all the pain you have gone through, after all the tears you have cried, on top of the victory God will also give you **joy**. God will make you laugh again. Lamentations 3:23 says, "**Great is His faithfulness, His mercies begin afresh each morning**". A morning will also come in your situation, when you will see God's mercies. When you will be filled with joy and laughter again.

There is no situation that is above God's ability to overcome. Mark 10:27 says, "**Jesus looked at them intently and said, humanly speaking it is impossible. But not with God, all things are possible with God.**" Whatever it is – **depression, anxiety, trauma, rejection, sickness, disease** – God will rescue you from it. Rest assured that it will come to an end, because God always wins. **So, hold on to your faith in Him. He will rescue you, He will fill you up with joy and laughter during and after the storm.**

God already took you out of the storm through Jesus Christ. Jesus' death and resurrection already gave you victory. His blood secured **eternal redemption** for you. You will be laughing louder than your enemies and longer than them too. They thought they had defeated you. Little did they know that the **Lord Jesus Christ,** in Whom you trust, rose from the dead with your victory. And the same power that raised Him from the dead lives in you.

So, there is no situation that can bury you, because you will just rise again through **Jesus Christ**. There is **no way** depression can bury you because you will keep rising. This is because your **God** is a **faithful God** Who **never fails**. **He is the same yesterday, today and forever. Amen!**

CHAPTER 30

ALL GLORY TO GOD, FOREVER AND EVER, AMEN! (ROMANS 11:36)

When the battle ends, you will realise that it was never about you. You were not depressed because you were weak. It all happened for God's glory. For the victory He gave you, all glory goes to Him.

In Romans 11:36, the Word of God says, "**For everything comes from Him, it is by His Power, and it is intended for His Glory. All Glory to Him Forever, Amen!**" This means that, whatever you went through, what you are going through right now and what you will go through in your life, victory is already given for His Name to be glorified. Trust God: **He will never fail you**. The victory He gave you is for His glory; there is no way He can fail Himself, there is no way He can fail you. You have already won the battle. Rejoice in the Lord. Receive this victory through faith and glorify His Name!

All Glory to God forever and ever. Amen!

www.ingramcontent.com/pod-product-compliance
Lightning Source LLC
Chambersburg PA
CBHW021937040426
42448CB00008B/1118